Be the Change

Nothing happens overnight when it comes to major changes. Usually it's so gradual that you hardly notice until the thing you remembered becomes something utterly different.

With personal changes, it's difficult to invest in change. You know something's possible and will probably only take 30 minutes a day to complete, but committing to do so when you have an ever changing schedule is something that's just too much to bear.

Well, you aren't alone. We all feel this way. And we can all do better. No reason to beat yourself up - we're all in this together. What you can do, though, is be the change you're looking to see in the world.

You can stop thinking about the specific things you want to be different about yourself currently. Think instead about the large things you want to change about the world and then do small things to work toward that change.

You'll find the size of the actions are the same, but the view and the outcome couldn't be more different. When you have a context for your actions bigger than just yourself, you can feel a part of something - a movement or a turning of the tide.

People crave these feelings more than they crave doing the same old routine. Religions would have far fewer adherents if this weren't the case. AA wouldn't exist either.

Find your bigger reason and model your behavior accordingly. Be the change you want to see in the world, and despite the silliness of the saying, I think you're going to like the change you see.

Cold Calling is Definitely Not Dead

If you hop on any job board and look for sales positions, which is a common practice for salespeople, you'll notice a theme with most job postings… **No Cold Calls Required.** The truth is, most people that have held a sales potion can sympathize with not wanting to do cold calls. With good reason- they're not fun, they're uncomfortable, and put most of your successes or failures as a salesperson squarely on your shoulders.

That last one is a big one. Most people are not bold by nature. They don't want to feel the weight of their personal success or failure. That's the difference when it comes to salespeople. When it's do or die, when the game is on the line, they want the ball.

Most of the best salespeople get into this line of work because they want the autonomy to control their financial and career success. When you take out marketing, networking, and cold calling and you rely on only passive leads, you remove the autonomy from the position. At this point, you're no longer selling a product, you're offering it.

Cold calling, whether on the phone or going out and knocking on doors, still generates more business and builds more long term business relationships than just putting a website out there and waiting for people to come and ask about your product. Some of the best advice we can give you as a salesperson is to get comfortable with being uncomfortable and get used to cold calling. It may not be fun but there's a reason that it's still around. At the end of the day, while warm leads are great, cold calling is going to help you increase your pipeline and drive sales.

Creating A Team Selling Atmosphere

Team selling is more impactful than individual salespeople going it alone. Being an island or a single star as a salesperson is less collaborative and less successful across the board than an archipelago or constellation of salespeople. Still more effective is a continent or galaxy of salespeople, making a large structure with a common purpose.

Many find themselves with a sales team that is secretive or in direct competition for clients. This is how most sales teams operate. Each salesperson is isolated and independent.

The typical way of paying salespeople usually works against the team idea. They are incentivized to not play well with others and keep to themselves.

Sharing is caring. Properly incentivizing collaboration is the best solution. Pay the sales team to truly be a team. Split sales, encourage lead sharing, and build a structure to reward fair play.

A rising tide raises all boats. When teams work together, everyone gets better, and sales productivity goes way up. Stop relying on the single salesperson to figure everything out on their own.

Give your sales team the tools they need to succeed and you'll lower your hiring costs, increase retention, and increase your sales.

Don't Fear The Teacher

The student will eventually become the teacher. As long as the student sticks around long enough to learn the hard lessons. This is what you want to happen.

The end goal of leadership in business is to replace yourself. It's a difficult thing to do well. It takes confidence and certainty and clarity of vision to choose the person most suited to your position when you can no longer do the work or get promoted.

Give your employees chances to grow into more challenging roles with more responsibility. They may enjoy this or hate it, but it'll help you earmark who can make the changes over time to become the future leader you need to fill your shoes.

Don't be afraid of your salespeople. Don't give them a reason to fear you. The relationship is a two way street, and one that should be mutually beneficial. Help them to do their best and teach them how to lead.

When you've trained them in the way they should go, you may just find that they stick to it and become the teacher you need them to be.

Do Something

Don't wonder what could happen. Don't see great things and let them pass you by. Don't wait for life to do something interesting.

Do something. Almost anything. Don't hurt anybody or take anything away from someone, but generally anything that doesn't do harm is better than doing nothing when it comes to achieving success.

It doesn't take a lot to do something. Very little in fact. Every little something counts. There are no somethings that count for nothing. Do something. Anything. Get to it.

Seriously, small commitments lead to bigger commitments. This is true for customers, but it's true for you as well. Commit to do small things. This builds trust in yourself and your power to achieve.

Slowly but surely you can grow that into bigger things. Be careful not to rush too fast into huge commitments and things to do. Usually you do big stuff a couple times max and then never want to do them again. Save the big things for later. Let's tackle the hills before the mountains.

Once you grow this small commitment into a larger one, you'll find you might actually trust yourself to get out there and achieve. You'll have real victories to point to, albeit small ones. Over time you really may be able to tackle the larger mountains in your life.

Dressing For Success

If you've been in sales for any amount of time, you've heard someone tell you something along the lines of "Invest in your wardrobe," "Dress for success," or "Dress for the job you want, not the job you have." As a young salesperson, I hated hearing this. I owned two cheap suits, and to me, this sounded like older people with more money than I had, making fun of me. It also bothered me that they thought that I needed to be super dressed up to make a sale. Years later, as I reflect on the situation, I realize that this was not the case.

Nobody was looking down on me or making fun of me, and they definitely were not saying that I needed to be dressed a certain way to make a sale. One thing that I overlooked, in all of my irritation, was that all of my counterparts had, more than likely, been in my shoes at the beginning of their sales career. They were just repeating what they had been told years before by someone else. It took me many years and a lot of wardrobe upgrades before I really grasped the meaning of what it meant to dress for success.

When I made my first career move into another industry outside of the automotive industry, I was surprised when I showed up to my first day, and no one was in a suit. Everyone was in jeans. I brushed it off as a casual office and went about my day. Then I was told that if I was gonna go out in the field that I needed to need to make a wardrobe change. For this industry, I was overdressed, and it would come off as intimidating that I needed to "Dress for success." This was a massive smack to my ego, you know, because I knew I looked good.

After a day of going out to construction sites and oil and gas sites, it became apparent to me that even in jeans and a sports coat that I was definitely overdressed. It was something that created a barrier and made it harder to connect with the prospects that I was meeting with. That was just not how people dressed in their industry, and thank goodness for that - I was sweating bullets in a jacket on a construction site in 90-degree weather.

So, I accepted the fact that I would need to conform to my new industry standards. I went and bought some jeans and more appropriate shirts, and the next time I went out for a meeting, I didn't feel that barrier. My prospects opened up to me more readily and allowed me to make a real connection with them. That's what you're always striving for in sales. You have to be a chameleon of sorts, you need to blend into the group you're with, and make a real connection with them so you can uncover what they truly need help with. The easiest way to do that, when you are new to the industry, is to look the part.

Filler Words

We're all guilty of using filler words. It's an epidemic. It's a national pastime.

Filler words are a huge obstacle when it comes to establishing authority. You need to establish that you're an expert to your customers. Saying "like," "um," "uh," "and so on," and "you know," take a decent pitch and tank it.

Don't let this happen to you. It's so very avoidable.

It does take practice and patience to break the habit. Practice makes permanent, so you have to make sure you're practicing the right things. If you go at it with poor habits, you'll continue to get poor results.

Work on your pitch, refine your approach, and get your message across to your prospective client. The customer's perception is your reality, and that means you need to put your pitch in terms that they can understand.

Avoid jargon and industry insider terms. Keep your pauses silent and don't fill them with empty sounds and words that just take up space in a conversation.

Take a class or get a coach if you have a particular issue with this, but everyone should be role playing and practicing on their colleagues, family, and in the mirror or on video.

It takes discipline to really nail it, but it's the foundation of your business - and you want your foundation to be solid.

Run your lines, get them memorized, keep the filler words out of the equation, and be the expert that people trust to buy from.

Flatter Sales Organizations

The market is strong, but payroll is tight. Companies are outsourcing work that isn't profitable to manage in house and looking to cut middle management or superfluous levels of oversight with their sales teams. In this climate, paths for title change and promotions are less clear. The goals and expectations for lower level sales people to move up the ladder necessarily change when there ceases to be a ladder or the ladder only has two rungs.

Where does this leave leaders who run sales departments or small companies? How can you motivate people when the promotion carrot becomes an empty dream, a mirage that loses substance when you get closer?

The answer is driving personal and professional growth in your sales team and deemphasizing promotions as a path to success. Supporting each salesperson and creating an atmosphere where teamwork is possible and profitable to each individual member of your team is key. Encouraging collaboration and properly incentivizing productive, revenue-generating habits increases the outcomes of your sales team.

Investing in your team is a personal choice. There is no need to cater to a select few, no need to send employees to expensive training sessions that they forget almost as soon as they get back in market, no need to replace your sales team, and no need to bang your head against the wall trying to communicate the need for improvement to disengaged salespeople. Nothing can be substituted for regular personal engagement on an individual level by a proven leader acting as a guide for your team to show the way to future growth.

In this era of increasingly flatter organizations, many at the not too distant top are realizing that they don't have the budget to hire a sales manager for their team or the skill set to manage sales professionals in a meaningful way. Luckily, there's an answer for that. Outsourcing is a major trend and most companies are familiar with outsourced human resources, sales, accounting, and other solutions, but few have been introduced to outsourced sales management. Having a part-time sales manager to guide your team to success without having to pay for a full-time sales manager may be the solution.

Get To The Point!

It's an often used phrase, but it has real truth to it. It's bad policy to lead with all the information the first time you talk to someone. It's also no good if you ramble on in successive meetings with people.

The truth is plain and simple, though that doesn't always make it simple to do - Get to the Point! Always come with a plan, with a strategy, with a "Point" to your interactions with people. Prospective or current customers are busy people with other things they see as more important to deal with.

Give them the courtesy of preparing and practicing your pitch and getting it out there for them to process. Don't get word vomit and talk prospective customers to death. You're much more likely to talk someone out of a sale than convince them to buy that way.

Lead with your basic idea and have answers at the ready for the questions you anticipate they may ask. Don't go into long answers or explanations. Just address their main concerns and get out.

There's a saying I love that is so true: Be Bright, Be Brief, Be Gone. Basically you should be memorable for the right reasons, get to the point, and get out. Remember to get on with it, and Get to the Point!

Get Top Talent Young

There's an open secret in business. Most people know about it, but they don't know how to apply it to their business. Young professionals are cheaper, more flexible, and have fewer bad habits than seasoned and top performing sales people.

Top talent can be molded into the sales force of your dreams of you get them young, and truly invest in their growth. When they grow and you see how they perform over time, you can earmark future leaders.

The idea is to replace yourself eventually in business so that the business can keep running when you leave. Sales people need time and attention, but some can fill their manager's shoes one day.

But it's not usually the ones you'd think it should be. Top performing salespeople should usually stay salespeople. Salespeople rarely make great managers. Often this is due to neglect in their prime training years, so start training early.

Get em young when you can still afford them and help them to grow alongside your business, gaining money as the company gains money. Company loyalty is mostly dead, but it can live on within your business if you want it to. If you properly incentivize these young people, they're likely to stick around and keep making you successful.

How Should I Manage My Calendar?

This is always a popular topic at the conferences and training events you might attend. With that in mind, we're willing to bet that most readers have had some sort of training on how to build a more efficient calendar to help manage their time.

It usually involves some extremely upbeat instructor showing screenshots of colorful blocks filling up an imaginary calendar. Then they'll tell you that you need to add every single thing from to meetings to bathroom breaks. Then we all clap and everyone walks away feeling optimistic about how organized they will be with their calendar when they get back. Then no one does anything about it.

I'm as guilty as anyone. I've been to tons of sessions on managing your time over the years. I've had some good takeaways that stuck. Do I have a beautifully organized calendar filled with vibrantly colored blocks that say what I'm doing every 15 minutes of every day? No, no, I do not. I do have a very well structured calendar that keeps me very well organized without putting a huge amount of time to manage the calendar itself.

When advising people, and in particular, salespeople, on how to structure their calendars, I generally give them some simple advice. You need to break your week into three major categories that make up most sales professionals' week.
1. Administrative/Office Time
2. Sales Calls/Meetings
3. Down Time

After years of managing my time and helping others manage their time for almost as long, I find that these are the three big categories for almost all salespeople. Once you realize this pattern, it becomes very easy to build a calendar that basically requires no upkeep. Boiling it down to simple terms and building your calendar around these three simple designations will help you create your best calendar life.

To give you an example, I'll start with my Administrative/Office Time. These require the least amount of effort because they don't change day to day. I'll set up the time that I need to do all my office work and the weekly internal meetings we have at SWC. Once I have them set and put them on repeat every week they become the nonnegotiables that I build the rest of my time around.

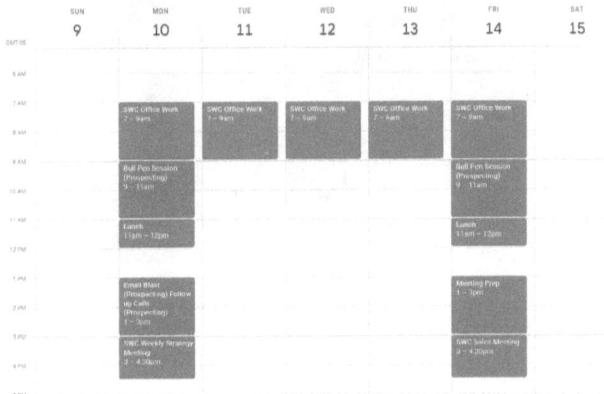

Once These recurring events are set I don't have to think about them. The very rarely have to change, and because of this, I spend very little time checking my calendar to see what I have coming up when I'm in the office.

The second category is sales calls and meetings. These are more room to play and can be moved around. I structure my calendar so that my midweek days are the days that I go out on meetings, sales calls, and cold calls. These events will change from week to week if not day to day.

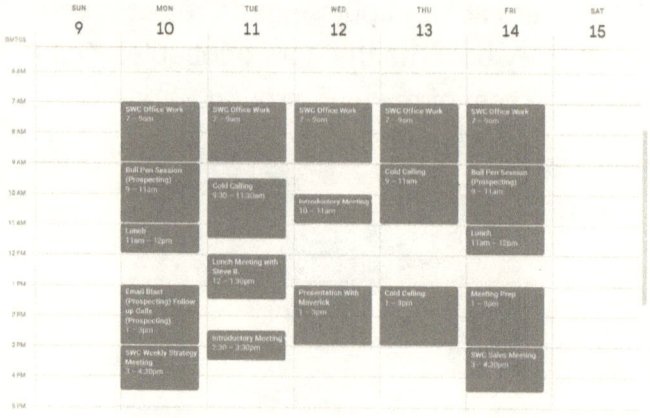

The last section is the most pliable of all it will change the day of or sometimes the hour of but to me, it is the most important for a salesperson to really plan out. It's your downtime. I try to be very intentional with my downtime. Work life balance is very important to any professional, but in a sales career, it can make or break you.

Sales is stressful, high pressure, and unforgiving. If you don't make time for downtime you'll burn out. I've watched it happen to so many people. I've gone through it myself, and discovered that my downtime was the most important thing that I added to my schedule. With that in mind, I'm very intentional with my downtime. I don't want to go home for the weekend and look up and realize that the weekend went by and I didn't do anything that I wanted to do.

Being intentional with your downtime is in investment in your health, your family, your career, and your happiness. So this is the one area of your calendar where I'd urge you to spend some time and really plan out what you want to do with your precious downtime.

Here's an example of what mine looks like.

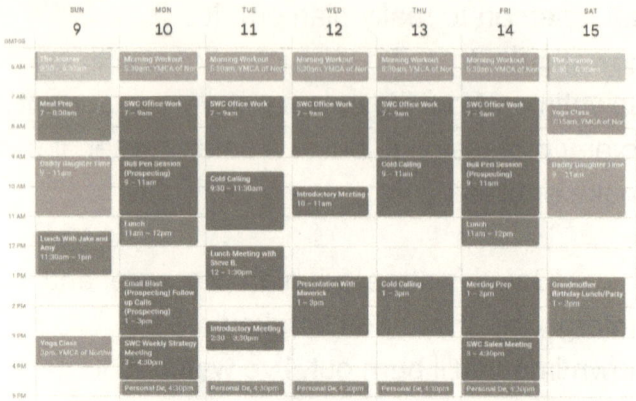

Wow, that looks really busy!

When everything is on it, your calendar will probably end up looking super full. Don't get overwhelmed by that though. Most of these are reoccurring events that will be on autopilot. In my calendar, 74% of those events are reoccurring at the same times every week.

Back to the main point, we've found that the best way to organize your calendar is into these three main categories.

Administrative/Office Time: This is the backbone of your work week. This is your time that you need to prep and complete everything internal so that when you're in the field making a pitch you're firing on all cylinders. These should almost all be reoccurring events that very rarely change.

Sales Calls/Meetings: As a salesperson, this will be all the time that you spend in the field, either knocking on doors making cold calls, or having meetings with prospects/clients. These times should be scheduled around you Administrative/Office time. Remember, you need that office time to make sure you're prepared to go out into the field if you run into a client you can't meet on a given week outside of your office time. Let them know you're booked up, and they'll respect that. After all you're busy and your time as a professional is valuable.

Downtime: This is often the most overlooked part of a calendar, can't be overlooked. Your downtime is what prevents burnout, and let's be honest, we all work to make a living - we don't live to work. With that in mind, you need to get almost greedy with your downtime. You need to be very intentional with it to make sure that you're getting the most out of your free time and living your best life.

How to Leave a Voice Mail That Will Get You a Call Back

One thing that you will often hear in sales is people grumbling that they have left a dozen messages for someone and they never hear back from them. If you've been a salesperson, at some point you've more than likely complained about this too. Why don't they call you back and how do you sound compelling enough to get a return call in a voicemail?

They don't call back for a lot of reasons, but the two main ones are that most decision makers (DM) get hundreds of sales calls a week and they don't have time to answer all of them. The second is that they know you're a salesperson and they don't want to invest their time just to hear your pitch. So, how does anyone get a call back? In part, it's a matter of persistence, professionalism, and creating urgency through a voicemail.

The first thing you want to do is be persistent. It does happen on occasion that you get a DM the first time that you call, or you get a call back the first time that you leave a voicemail, but in almost every case this won't be how it goes. Most of the time you'll need to put in multiple calls. Sometimes you'll have to put in dozens to get a DM on the line, and over time if you continue to leave voicemails, that same DM will see that you're putting in a lot of work to get their attention. This will make them more likely to answer when you call and more likely to give you a callback.

The second thing you want to do is be professional. You're not the only one trying to get a DM's attention, so you need to distinguish yourself. How do you make yourself sound more professional over a voicemail, though? The best way is to know what you're going to say if you get your prospect's voicemail before you ever call them. I always recommend that you have a standard script for voice mails when you're cold calling. Something like the following:

"Hello John, This is Mike Smith with SWC Sales Management. It's around 8 AM on Tuesday the 11th and I am reaching out to talk to you about what I do for Company A, B, and C. If you could give me a call back on my cell phone at (713) 478-3298, it would be great to speak with you, and I'll plan on giving you a call back this coming Thursday the 13th if I don't hear back from you sooner. Have a great rest of your day and I look forward to speaking with you soon."

The third and final way to increase the likelihood of someone calling you back is to create urgency. Don't worry, you won't have to shout into the phone about how you're having a sale that's only lasting till the end of the week. You're not trying to create urgency to close the deal at the moment. You're trying to create a little urgency to have the DM call you back. That's where those last two sentences in my voicemail script really come into play.

You've already established your professionalism in the message you left prior to that. So they know who you are and that you're not just spamming his inbox. You've let them know that you work with other people in the area and that you want to share some best practices that you have with them and can share. Now you've created some urgency by stating that you were going to give him a call back on a specific date.

Knowing that you've called before, that you plan to call back, and that you do work with other companies in the area, will create a sense of urgency with a lot of decision makers. They don't want to ignore you if you work with others in their industry, and they'll often want to get ahead of you calling back if they have free time to actually speak to you.

With these three components: Persistence, Professionalism, and Urgency, you'll increase the likelihood of a prospect calling you back tremendously.

Invest, Don't Replace

Hiring is expensive, time consuming, and frustrating. Finding and onboarding new talent can often be replaced by investing in the team you already have.

It's a classic "grass is always greener on the other side" scenario. You see the faults in your sales team and dream of what could be out there, just waiting to be found. Paying attention and investing in the people right in front of you can lead to much better results.

People don't leave jobs, they leave their managers. A salesperson's direct report may be a traditional sales manager with responsibility for their own ledger, a former top performer that moves into a management role, or a business owner performing multiple roles. In any structure, getting regular, measurable, feedback and having someone that listens and advocates for their sales team drives retention and productivity.

There's a positive correlation between retention and productivity when sales teams are managed to their full potential. Making sure top performers aren't the only ones that get attention or facetime is key. The accepted rule that 80% of your sales are driven by 20% of your sales team doesn't have to apply here. The rest of the team is just as valuable as your top performers if they're invested in properly.

If your lowest performers are made into better than average performers, sales for the company goes way up. A rising tide raises all boats. There are no members of a sales team that are unimportant. The ones that seem the least worthwhile are the ones that need the most guidance.

If you don't have the time to invest in your team, find someone who does. Strategic Sales Management may be a solution you haven't considered yet. If you have, maybe it's time to reach out to someone who can make your weakest performers into salespeople you can count on.

Keep at it - the Grind

It's fun when things go well and when you're busy. It's great when business is booming. Inevitably, though, you will hit a slump. It's important that you've done the right things while you're busy and experiencing success, so you can keep operating and possibly thriving during the slow times.

It can be a grind to do so. When you're busy, it's hard to prioritize your time. Chances are, there's some administrative or customer related task that is more urgent than marketing or networking or sales calls.

When you feel this way, just remember to keep at it. You're laying the groundwork for success when you need it the most. It's a sales rainy day fund. It's a savings plan for your business. You've already put a lot of sweat equity and money on the line - it's worth that little more to protect your investment.

When it feels the least worth it, just remember that it's not about that moment, it's about the seed that's planted in that moment that will grow into something bigger.

Insure your success by keeping at it, even when it feels like a grind.

Key To Management

The key elements to successful teamwork are trust, communication and effective leadership. There are key elements to each of these categories as well, but we're going to stick to the key to management.

Here at SWC, we're experienced management professionals. We've done the things that lead to success and made the mistakes that help us learn, and we pass this experience on.

Management, especially in sales, is a difficult balance.

You have to consider your team and your place in it. As a leader, everything you do directly affects how your team performs and goes about their daily tasks.

If you can do these next few things, you'll greatly increase your chances of success:

- Communicate Clearly
- Manage Your Team's Time
- Facilitate Teamwork & Collaboration
- Delegate Tasks to Promote Development
- Solve Problems With Your Team
- Set Team Goals & Analyze Results
- Develop Your Emotional Intelligence

- Be Tactful in Your Transparency

Using a measurable and duplicatable sales process across top and low performers replaces the reliance on any one person or group and leads to significantly better results.

When sales professionals have clear objectives (communication), leadership (effective), and accountability (trust), revenue increases across the board.

Become the manager your team needs today.

Leadership and Sales 12 month Reading List

Several years ago, when I was starting down my career path, I decided I wanted to try and give myself a crash course in leadership and sales training. I was too broke to go to a lot of seminars or conferences on the subject, so I turned to what I could afford. I went online and looked up as may "top ten leadership books lists" as I could find. From that, I created a reading list of books I saw repeated on most of the other lists as well as a few that sounded interesting to me.

As SWC approaches the beginning of our new fiscal year, we decided to put a 12-month reading list to get the year going. When I did this years ago, I found it very enlightening, and if you decide to commit to completing this 12-month journey, we feel strongly that it will be similarly impactful for you.

1. On Fire: The 7 Choices to Ignite a Radically Inspired Life

2. Primal Leadership: Realizing the Power of Emotional Intelligence

3. Team of Rivals: The Political Genius of Abraham Lincoln

4. The Truth about Leadership: The No-fads, Heart-of-the-Matter Facts You Need to Know

5. How to Win Friends & Influence People

6. [Endurance: Shackleton's Incredible Voyage](#)

7. [Good to Great: Why Some Companies Make the Leap and Others Don't](#)

8. [The Obstacle Is the Way: The Timeless Art of Turning Trials into Triumph](#)

9. [The Emperor's Handbook: A New Translation of The Meditations](#)

10. [The Achievement Habit: Stop Wishing, Start Doing, and Take Command of Your Life](#)

11. [Rebel Talent: Why It Pays to Break the Rules at Work and in Life](#)

12. [The Five Dysfunctions of a Team: A Leadership Fable](#)

We're very excited about taking on the 12-month challenge, and we hope you join us. If you do, make sure to send us a message or a comment along the way, to let us know how it's going. Best of luck, and I hope this helps you push your leadership and sales acumen to the next level.

Leverage your life

Personal experiences go hand in hand with work accomplishments. It's not just about your work history any more than college applications are about grades. It's all about the extracurricular activities.

Let people know what you're into. Talk about the sports team you were on back in the day, the hiking you enjoy with your family, and the shows or novels you like to watch, listen to, or read.

Keep doing the things you enjoy. It leads to moments where you can connect with your prospects and clients. Be transparent and let your true self shine through. Doing the things you love is contagious
In the same way that success and happiness are contagious too.

Find a hobby if you don't have one. Find something to be passionate about. Find something outside of work to give you a little bit of happiness.

When you give people you're background in business, add a caveat that includes what you do for fun. Find small ways to weave it into conversation.

Make sure you aren't inserting these facts about yourself at the wrong time. Intro's and ice breakers with people you've just met and people who you've already built some trust and relationship with are the best people to talk to about your personal life.

Stay away from this technique in high pressure negotiations, board meetings, presentations in front of a crowd, and etc. Usually it's a good lead in and sometimes can even help you relieve tension in certain situations.

Remember, when you leverage your life, you leverage your personal as well as professional experiences. Combined, that can make all the difference in making connections with clients and building the trust you need to close deals.

Listen First

Then Acknowledge, Explore, and Respond. It's a technique that is very common in healthcare and social work, but used less often than it should be in sales. It's called the LAER process, and like you may have guessed, it's an acronym.

I've already said what it stands for, so I'll break down what each category means instead.

Listen:
Listening is the MOST important skill you can have when understanding how to respond to someone's objections. Even though listen is the first step, it really applies to the entire process.

You must take active care to not interrupt, even though you may not agree.

When you actively listen, you show people that you respect how they feel. You also show that your response will take into account how they feel.

Acknowledge:
When it's your time to talk, always start with by acknowledging what you've just heard. It's so important that people know that what they're saying doesn't fall on deaf ears.

By acknowledging, you say, "I get that."

This doesn't mean you have to agree with your objector, but instead that you are meeting them at their concerns.

Acknowledging doesn't always need to be verbal. If you're face-to-face, a simple head nod at the right time can say, "I'm listening and understand."

Explore:

In my opinion, this is the step that most people miss. Consequently, it's also the most powerful step in the process. When you explore, you ask questions that allow you to better understand why people are objecting.

If you simply assume that you know why they don't agree, you will often only touch on the surface of their reasoning when you respond.

Here's where the ever powerful 'why' comes into play. By asking people why they are objecting, you uncover what makes them feel uncomfortable.

Here's the key, and HubSpot's Brooke Freedman said it best, "seek to understand, not to be right."

Go into the Explore process knowing that while you may not agree with the objections, the person objecting does. Your job at this point is not to align what you hear with your beliefs, but completely understand theirs so that you can respond them realistically.

Respond:

Here is everyone's most practiced part. The only difference now is you'll have all the information to respond to what actually matters based upon your following of the previous steps.

The key here isn't to tell someone why their way of thinking is wrong, but to lay out all the facts and let them determine what makes the most sense.

Mastering LAER

In a nutshell, proper LAER technique involves listening intently to what someone is saying, acknowledging that you understand their objections, exploring deeper what pain they envision that's driving that objection, and finally, when you fully understand the pain, responding to it.

Used correctly, and in the right order, those four techniques make for objection handling any salesperson should master.

Management Face Time

I'm not referring to a video call or chat. We're talking about real, quality face to face time with your managers. Between employees and their managers, do you know how much time there is planned for face to face conversations and coaching?

The national average is 39% of the day planned to be used for this purpose, according to the Harvard Business Review. The reality is much lower. Reported by the same institution, the average amount of time managers are able to get in front of their employees is 9% of their day to day work.

The good news is, more coaching is not necessarily better. In fact, it can be detrimental. Putting the wrong things or even too much of the right feedback into play with an employee, can drive production way down. Too much feedback causes interruptions in the regular workflow of any employee, but especially a salesperson.

Less and higher quality coaching and feedback are the true gold standard in management, especially sales management. Our company plans to spend 10% of any given week intensely focused on our clients' sales teams. This, it turns out, is the ideal amount of time to be effective in driving results, but staying out of the way of your employees' success.

Networking is the Best Form of Marketing

Going to events can be intimidating or feel like a waste of time, and to be sure, they sometimes are. It's still important to get out there and meet people. And it's as important you network the right way as it is for you to network in the first place.

Research shows that professional networks lead to more opportunities, advancement, innovation, knowledge, and status. Building professional relationships improves work quality and job satisfaction.

But it's still awkward. Nothing changes that. Just like you really have to make calls and conduct meetings and ask for sales to close deals - you have to network to leverage your expertise among your peers.

There are a few strategies. Most of them do involve an exchange of information, but best not to lead with the business card. This has a tendency to shut down conversation when conversation is the gas that keeps the networking engine running.

An easy approach is to stand near the food or drink being served. People will naturally be drawn to you.

Another approach is to stand in the middle or corner of the room by yourself. The negative space and your singular figure will draw people to you.

Some people are practically made of charm. These events are tailored for those people. Find a lane and stick to it. Play to your strengths.

Whatever you do, just remember - the more you network, the better you'll do in business. Take the time to invest in yourself and your career and build your network now.

Organize Your Life

Everyone would love to be organized. Some of you actually have this already nailed and really, you don't have much new to learn here if you are. The rest of you, though, know you need some help.

This isn't exactly like an issue like hoarding, but it isn't not an issue, right? Well, this is your intervention. Whether you clean up your living space or make your desk neat, these things are foundational to being successful.

It's hard to achieve great things when you can't see though your haze of stuff. Once you have the general spring cleaning done, keep it that way. I know that's easier said than done, but stick with it.

The next step is to organize your files. Throw out most of your stuff unless it's a business or personal record you absolutely must keep. What are the chances you would need or want to refer back to the notes of a meeting you took ten years ago? Slim to none, right? Toss 'em.

After that, you should organize the files on your computer and email. Create folders to file your different documents and emails and file each one away as you complete the associated task.

Once you're all cleaned up and have your files in order, organize your calendar. Keep it simple. Make three different categories and put each time into one of them: meetings/sales calls, admin/office work, and down time. Everything you do pretty much fits into these categories.

Nail these things and you'll have a mostly organized life. Fail and you'll just be where you're at. There's nothing to lose, so you might as well go ahead and get organized.

Overcoming Objections - Lean In

Objections can catch even seasoned salespeople off guard. They can be scary, heated, dismissive, and put you on your heels when you think a sale is going south.

The trick is, you have to play it cool. I know that's easier said than done. It certainly takes practice and time to get good at it.

It helps if you reframe the way you look at the objection and take it as an opportunity to impress your client. An objection isn't a no. It isn't the end of the conversation either. Objections are a way for the customer to tell you what problems they need solved that you haven't addressed well enough yet.

To put the client's fears to rest and get that sale, you have to do your homework. Make sure you know or research or ask more seasoned people in your industry what the common objections to your product or service are before you go into a meeting. Always come armed with answers to those issues and know you may get thrown a curveball.

It's okay not to have an answer to everything- if you don't know, tell them you'll find out and follow up appropriately. Never give answers to things you're unsure of or you'll chance getting caught.

In the end, objections are the final step before getting the sale. Don't let them hold you back. Lean in and show that you're prepared and aren't scared and close that deal!

Perfecting The Pitch

As sales professionals, usually talking isn't an issue. Talking is part and parcel of the job description, and chances are, you're already good at that. The difference between a decent pitch and a great one is small, but important.

The key is to be quick, concise, and memorable. Then shut up or leave, depending on the situation. Rambling loses time and attention and leaves a less desirable impression.

In some cases, you need to delve deep and nurture a relationship as you navigate a long sales process. In this case, your pitch is broad and brief to get your foot in the door. At the end of the process your final pitch is more precise and dialed in and may include more personal conversation.

Any sales situation includes a pitch, but it's important not to sound canned. Learn the information that matters to your customers and refine your approach. Lead with the most important information and don't get lost in the weeds.

The more you practice, the more it'll stick, and you'll be more effective in the field. Whether you're in an elevator, an introductory meeting, or a closing presentation, your pitch will set you apart from the competition.

Process Not Person

Business leaders often rely on star performers and personalities and their quirks, to make sure sales keep coming in. They don't want to mess with the mojo of their top salespeople.

The issue with this idea is inconsistency. When you rely too strongly on any one person or group of people, you risk your company's future. Giving salespeople the power to determine the course of your destiny based on their mood and personal interests is almost always a mistake.

Giving your top performers too much latitude makes it increasingly more difficult over time to course correct or give constructive criticism. Treating your star performers with too much deference alienates the rest of your sales team and causes frustration and costly high turnover.

Using a measurable, duplicatable, and proven sales process across top and low performers replaces the reliance on any one person or group and leads to significantly better results. When sales professionals have clear objectives, leadership, and accountability, revenue increases across the board.

Rely on processes, not individual salespeople.

Processes don't have moods, crises, or home

issues to bring to work with them. Processes are concrete and reliable. Don't replace low performers and create a revolving process of hiring while relying on a select few. Drive everyone to succeed and build the team you have to get the results you need.

Replace Yourself

Everyone likes being the best and most important. It's hard sometimes to give others the recognition they deserve when you might look bad or lose out on something because of it. But the aim in business is to replace yourself.

In the short run, everything is mostly a competition. In the long game, you should be investing in relationships. You never know where relationships can take you. Who you know is almost always more important than what you do, though you better know what you're doing too.

When you invest in relationships, you find people to earmark for the future. You hand pick who you want ideally to run departments or locations or regions based on your plans for succession. Someone needs to be in place when you leave.

You need to have good people ready to step in when you're gone. You shouldn't leave your company in a bad situation. When you heavily invest in people, it gives returns on your investment ore quickly than you'd think.

This isn't just a 25-30 year plan. This can come back in just months or a few years. It's the connections and relationships with people that really pay off. Replace yourself and you may see a major return on that personal investment.

Say Yes To Ideas

Allow your employees the privilege of failure. Don't stifle growth by saying no too often. Boundaries are a necessary part of business and even life, but saying yes to ideas and giving your salespeople the room to make mistakes and learn from them, is important too.

Salespeople are usually go getters and self motivated and require less direction than most employees. Often they need reigning in and redirecting more than telling exactly what to do.

Make sure you aren't talking down to them and make sure you listen when they have an idea about how to succeed in the future.

Once you've listened, say yes. You don't have to let them have everything they want. Let's be honest, salespeople aren't always the most realistic bunch. Give them what they need to try out their idea without hurting themselves or others too seriously. Put parameters around their goals and expectations for how the idea should work.

Then let them work it out. If it fails, give them the critical feedback to let them know the score and how they can improve the next time. If they succeed, you may have a new sales process or method to spread to the rest of your team. Either way, you get buy in from your team and cultivate the behaviors a successful salesperson needs to succeed.

It all starts when you say yes.

Snap Email Marketing

I could not tell you exactly who first introduced me to the concept of "snap emails," but it changed the way I structure my email marketing forever. The basic idea is that your email should be so concise and to the point that if some were to receive it on their smartphone that they could read it in as if it were a personal text message. It seems to be silly, but I got more traction in my marketing campaigns by sending out less info than I ever did with sending out big long emails full of free information.

When I was first introduced to this style of email, I was told to treat an email like a tweet, try to keep it to 140 characters or less. This would allow the prospect to read the email in a few seconds when they glance down to quickly check their phone. I've since adjusted a bit. When I send out a marketing email, my goal is to make sure that if that client were to check their email on the phone that they won't have to scroll down to finish reading. This allows me a little more leeway to make my emails look a tad more professional.

Before changing my email marketing strategy, I had very rarely received a call or an email back from one of my email blasts. Once I implemented this strategy, I started receiving back several responses every time I sent out a batch of emails. Which to me at the time was a game changer. Bellow is a quick example I sent to myself and a screenshot to give you a quick visual reference.

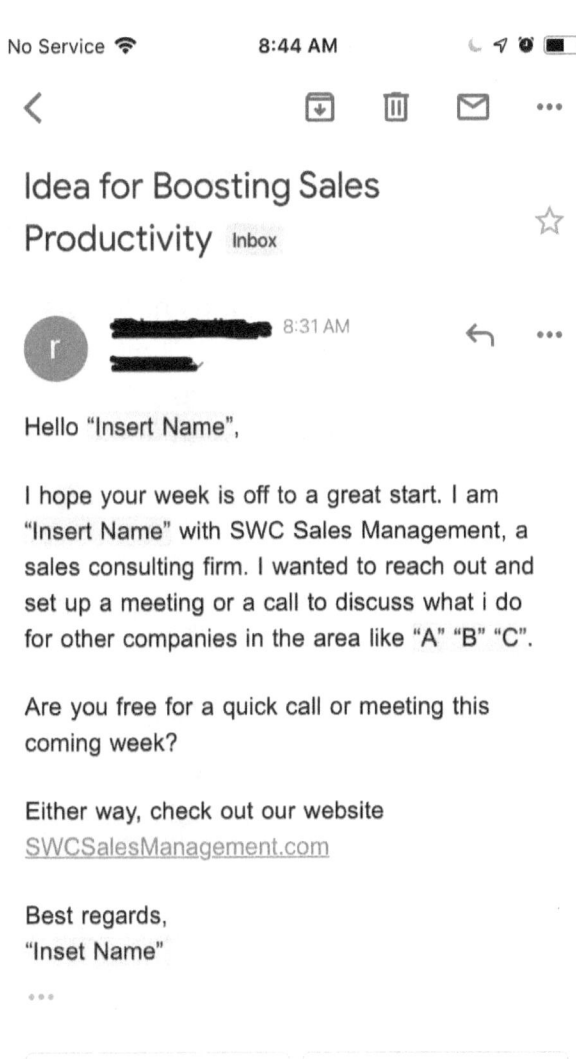

The reason that this works is how short and to the point the email is. You are in sales you are asking someone to take their attention away from what they are doing to make a living and to give it to you. If you want that attention you need to be to the point with them, and when it comes to emails - if they need to scroll to read the whole message they'll move on. You asking for their attention doesn't take precedence over what they need to do, day to day, in their job.

Some People Just Aren't Managers

The title of the article is pretty self-explanatory. It's also very blunt, but it is the truth. Early on in my career and in most people's careers, you find that this is a hard concept to swallow. It is, however, something that everyone at some point in their working life has to come to terms with.

That was certainly something that I struggled with when I was in my first management position. My sales team consisted of four people. It wasn't the first time I was tasked with managing people, but it was the first time that I was graded on developing a sales team. It was a hard first few months, but we got the sales numbers above where they needed to be. The team worked better than it had in a long time. There was one thing that I just couldn't seem to get to work. Something that I couldn't motivate them to do.

I could not for the life of me to motivate any of them to take the next step and move up to manage their own sales team at another location. I could not wrap my head around why they wouldn't want to progress in their career path. Then I finally got one of them to take it seriously enough to interview to be a manager at one of our other locations.

SHE GOT THE JOB! HOORAY!

She hated it…

Boo…

She hated her new role. She didn't like managing people. She didn't like the pressure, and ultimately, she didn't perform well.

She eventually left that role and started a new career path in accounting. I was happy for her, but I also couldn't understand why she didn't like her managerial position. I couldn't wrap my head around why she didn't perform like I knew that she could, and it made me feel like I had failed her. Pushed her into a role she wasn't ready for.

It took a long time for me to come to terms with the fact that I hadn't failed her and that she hadn't failed herself. She just was not cut out for that role. She was cut out for a career in accounting. This is something that I can see now in retrospect, and something that I try to look for when I manage people. When someone on the team is not just capable of taking my place but will enjoy that position, thrive under its pressures, and will, in the end, be Succesful, I needed to replace myself as the sales manager.

Often times it's not the top performer on your team. Usually, it's the employee in the middle of the pack that's the best team player. It's a quality that's hard to put into words, but in a team environment, anyone can spot that person. My problem at the time was looking at my sales team and pushing the best salespeople to be managers, when I should've been looking at my team and driving the best potential managers to be salespeople until they were ready to make the jump into the next step in their career.

Not everyone is going to be a successful manager, and not everyone wants to be. What I've learned is that if you push someone who's not right for management (even if they're capable) into that role, they'll struggle and it'll make them disengaged. If you are really honest with them, they'll more than likely be able to tell you that they didn't want to be in that role in the first place.

So the take away here, the "So What?" is that it's okay that not everyone is cut out for management. It's okay if some people want to be life long salespeople, or accountants, or receptionists. Being uncomfortable is good- it promotes growth, but if you push someone to grow in the wrong area to fit your agenda, it's doing them a disservice.

The Gatekeeper is Your Friend

There's a common misconception that gatekeepers are our enemy, people to get around or trick to get a sale. Gatekeepers are people too. They're more than secretaries, office administrators, and low level employees. They have wants and desires and stories to tell.

Engaging and truly listening to the people who are between you and the decision maker that you need to make that sale, is often the difference between being a highly effective salesperson and a merely adequate salesperson. Never look past the front desk associate when calling on a business in person. Speak to them, ask them how their day is going, and give them your full attention before asking who to contact to make a decision on your product or service. When on the phone, give them attention without spending too long on introductions or wasting their time, but still give them the opportunity to speak about themselves before asking for information.

Gatekeepers can get you the information you need. Make no mistake, they know who you need to reach out to. They're trained to keep time wasters out of the reach of their bosses. Differentiate yourself by being a decent person to them first, then ask for their help.

Asking is the next important step, and how you ask can make a huge difference. Let them know you don't want to waste anyone's time, but you need help knowing who to reach out to about the issue your product or service solves. See if they can point you in the right direction.

If you've done the introduction and ask well, you're more than likely going to get the information you need to succeed. This doesn't mean you'll get the information every time. People have bad days and might just not like the sound of your voice. But you'll find that gatekeepers aren't so difficult to deal with, more often than not, when you treat them like the people they really are.

The Most Important Lesson in Sales

I have spent most of my working adult life in some form of sales. Throughout my career, from retail in a brick-and-mortar store, to business-to-business sales (B2B), making pitches to C suite executives, I have learned a lot of lessons on how to present my message and manage the sales process.

One lesson particularly stands out to me head and shoulders above the rest, and if you've been in sales, you'll probably recognize it:

"You can't lose business you don't have."

It sounds so simple and intuitive, but for me, hearing this was truly a turning point in how I approach sales. When I was working in retail, there was no time to think about winning or losing a sale. Transactions were quick, usually only lasting a few minutes. Sometimes, they would extend into two or more days if it was a big purchase, but they were, as a rule of thumb, to the point and over with very quickly.

In contrast, in B2B sales, a short sales process was 30 days and a long one could take 90 or more. In addition to that, you might get the same amount of sales opportunities in one month as you do during a single day in retail. Once I realized this, I suddenly became much more aware of how limited my chances were to land a deal.

As a result, I was in my own head before every meeting. Worry would immediately set in. I was afraid I was going to ruin the opportunity to bring a new client on board. So naturally in every meeting anxiety would take over and my reaction was overwhelming.

My mouth would dry out, I would get hot and start to sweat, and a knot would form in the pit of my stomach. Worse than that, once in the meeting, I would be noticeably flustered and apprehensive, stay quiet and not challenge customer for fear of saying the wrong thing or pushing too hard for a commitment. As a result, I probably lost out on some business that I shouldn't have.

This must have been pretty apparent to not only my potential clientele, but also to my Sales Manager. Thankfully, he stepped in and helped me correct my issues before they got out of hand. The problem was affecting my confidence, and I truly don't know if I could have overcome it so quickly without his intervention. This is why it's so important to have someone on your team dedicated to developing your salespeople, not just looking at spreadsheets and setting goals.

My Sales Manager brought the issue up to me in one of our meetings and tried to help in a number of ways. We ran through several role plays and talked through the problem. In the end, he gave me a piece of advice that took several months to take hold, but when it finally took root, completely changed my view of every cold call and meeting I had.

"You can't lose business you don't have"

Once that finally got through to me, and I realized that I didn't have anything to lose, I was able to relax and be myself. I came into my own as a B2B salesperson. I was more willing to ask hard questions and push potential clients to for a commitment and I wasn't worried about walking away from business that wasn't really there to begin with.

The two big takeaways from this story are pretty simple. The first is that in your sales career you have to have a great mentor or manager to help you develop and push you to to be the successful salesperson that you want to be. The second, and to me the most important, lesson you can learn in sales is...**"You can't lose business you don't have".**

Transfer of Trait

You practice how you play, are what you eat, and fake it 'till you become it. These are ideas most people are aware of. Another is to raise your child in the way they should go, and when they're old, they won't depart from it. It's an odd thing to say, but when you're a leader, you have a similar responsibility to a parent.

You're the example, the standard, the measure by which all others are judged. The power part of this is attractive to a lot of people. Unfortunately, when people are attracted to the power, but not the responsibility, they make for poor leaders. The same is true for people who are given responsibility but not the power to do anything. They're inextricably bound together.

You have an outsized influence on your employees. What you do, they will do. What you allow, they will allow. It's important to keep the standards for yourself high to make sure your team's output is high.

If it sounds hard, that's because it is. But it's worth it.

In the end the results your team brings in are going to far outpace the extra effort you give if you truly commit. The traits you show on a regular basis transfer to your team. Make sure the traits you transfer are the right ones.

Vision is Key

Organizations can operate and make money without vision. Plenty of companies get by without a cohesive initiative shared from top to bottom and throughout all positions. They do fine by going through the repetitive motions that have worked for them in the past.

An object in motion tends to stay in motion . . . unless acted upon by an outside force.

And as we know, the market is ever changing and likely to provide the outside force that upturns a business that once was perfectly profitable.

This is necessarily a path to eventual failure. A wheel with nothing to guide it will roll for a while, but eventually hit a wall. A wheel connected to a car can effectively be steered to hopefully avoid long term disaster.

Both methods involve moving forward, but the approach couldn't be more different.

Creating and communicating a clear vision for your company is essential.

Making sure your sales team, customer service, operations, and management are all on the same page and understand their role in the larger scale of the operation creates an efficient vehicle for success. Driving revenue once this vehicle is tuned up becomes significantly smoother.

Having the right management roles to disseminate your message from the top to your direct performers is the step where most businesses lose their way. This is particularly true with your sales team. If the revenue producers aren't properly incentivized or don't understand your vision, they're going to head in a direction that you didn't intend, like a car that needs an alignment.

Keep your producers and your vision aligned with strategic sales management and make sure you're heading into the future you want, where the rubber meets the road.

Why Your Sales Team Needs A CRM

Anyone who has been involved with the implementation process of a Customer Relationship Management "CRM" program, knows the frustration that comes along with it. We certainly see this all the time, but even though it's frustrating, you've got to stick with it. In time, once your team has fully adopted the practice, they won't know how they got anything done before they had a CRM.

The big thing to keep in mind when adopting a CRM is to focus on all the ways that it'll make your teams' work lives more manageable. When you keep that as the focus, you can easily overcome the frustration your team will experience during the adoption phase. Let's walk through some of the most significant benefits of utilizing a CRM.

<u>Centralized storage all of your customer data:</u>

If you've ever had someone on your sales team call you and ask to find a business card somewhere in a stack of 200 they have on their desk so you can send them a name or a number, then this will be huge. If you have a CRM in place and you need to find any data you have about your clientele, as long as you have access to your computer or your phone, it's right at your fingertips. You can almost instantly pull up any data you need about your client from simple things like names, phone numbers, or email addresses, to more complex info you may need to strategize before a meeting, like invoices, contracts, and agreements.

Improve communication across the organization:

This will be huge for your support team. Let's say you have a presentation that you need to put together and you need data from several different team members. If you have several people involved, you can create a task with due dates for everyone to compete within the CRM. Once they complete them, they can store them in a customer's account, where your salesperson that's presenting can compile all the data and create their presentation.

Makes Management's life easier:

Speaking from the perspective of a manager, this one is huge. Being able to look in and see all of your salespeoples' pipelines and opportunities and see exactly where they are in the sales process at any given time. It's an incredibly powerful tool. It allows you to make more accurate projections, know how you can help your salespeople accelerate their closes, and will enable you to see when and where you need to step in and help. The transparency that a CRM brings to the sales team may be the most potent attribute it offers. This transparency allows manager insight which helps you to develop your team and ultimately provide a better service to your clientele.

Makes your sales team's life easier:

Aside from the ease with which a CRM allows your sales team to access data, the comment I hear most often from salespeople, is the transparency that a CRM creates. Most organizations have at least one person that approaches a CRM with skepticism. They view it as a tool for someone to micromanage them. That's a fair view if you've never used one before, but if a CRM is being used properly, this view couldn't be further from the truth.

It actually allows your salespeople more freedom to work without management calling or emailing them for updates several times per day. Instead, if everything is being entered into the CRM promptly, management can look in at any moment and see exactly where any salesperson is with any given prospect. This goes back to transparency, which we feel genuinely is the most significant benefit to having a CRM in place for your sales team.

If you don't have a CRM in place, we would strongly recommend looking into them. You might get a little push back at first, but good sales managers make the hard decisions and do what's best for the team and their organization. In the long term, your team will thank you once they adapt to the CRM.

Work Life Balance

This is a term that's thrown around a lot, but I don't think many people actually follow through on it. It's possible that people don't even really know what they mean by it. Without a good example, it's difficult to say what you want out of work and life together. It's a big question with no clear answer.

Work and life are symbiotic, but it's important that one doesn't overtake the other. If work becomes your life, you likely have a problem. Work can become a parasite and suck the life out of, well, your life.

I'd say it's not likely you'll find a fifty fifty balance and maybe not a sixty forty balance. But if at least 30% of your waking life isn't free of work obligations, you're cruisin' for a bruisin' or headed straight for burnout.

There are some recommendations on this subject. Keep your phone plugged in somewhere that isn't in your bedroom is a good start. Having a mandatory phone away time is also helpful. If you're an employer, waiting to ask questions until your workforce is at work is the best practice. Allow for downtime and rest. Don't monopolize your team's time.

If you can allow yourself and others the right to rest and recoup, you'll find productivity generally rises. It's all a balance, and like anything, it takes practice to get it right. Start now and put the slogan you've been saying or hearing to work. See what a difference work life balance can actually make.

You Need Experience

It's something everyone has heard about a job at some point. It's unfortunately true. You do need experience. Lucky for you, experience is generally attainable.

It's not an unlimited resource, but it is plentiful. If you're in a specific profession with licensure and hours of credit requirements, you're out of luck. The only way is the slow and steady way.

For the rest of you fine folks, there's a faster way. Still not fast by any means, but faster. The first thing is to do something. Just about anything. Work a job and keep working it for more than a year. Two is better.

Start young. Get a job at or before 18. Barring that, get one as soon as you can. Once you've worked a crappy job for a couple years, you can start applying to slightly better jobs. We're talking professional, but not great jobs here. If you're a college graduate, that makes this process a whole lot easier, as long as you work some through school (preferably consistently).

Once you've had that professional but entry level job, stay there. Try to do your job as well as it can be done. Stay there some more. Try to get promoted. After you've been there five to seven years, look for a better job if you aren't getting the advancement or opportunities you desire or need.

Once you've followed these few steps, your future prospects of employment open up. You've established your credibility as a trusted business person. Now just keep it up and keep following the process.

www.ingramcontent.com/pod-product-compliance
Lightning Source LLC
Chambersburg PA
CBHW030729180526
45157CB00008BA/3099